HODDER ENGLIS

This book includes a variety of activities for individuals and groups that will guide you through the text, treating *Macbeth* as a play written for performance. The aim is to help you to understand a Shakespeare text in detail, and to prepare you for the kind of course work assignments on which you will be assessed. You will develop your skills as:

SPEAKERS AND LISTENERS

by discussing the meaning of key scenes and speeches
by analysing the motivation of the main characters and voicing their thoughts
by debating differences of interpretation
by mounting a trial in order to investigate the death of Duncan

READERS

by studying key scenes and reading between the lines
by finding evidence from the text to support a point of view
by exploring the impact of the images with which the play is studded

WRITERS

by writing about the characters
by making notes for a theatre director, and offering advice to the actors
by penning a declaration to James I, justifying the inclusion of the witches
by producing course work assignments

THE ROAD TO MADNESS AND DESPAIR

In the final act of the play, Macbeth reveals his feelings about life; its total emptiness and lack of meaning.

To-morrow, and to-morrow, and to-morrow
Creeps in this petty pace from day to day,
To the last syllable of recorded time;
And all our yesterdays have lighted fools
The way to dusty death. Out, out brief candle!
Life's but a walking shadow, a poor player
That struts and frets his hour upon the stage,
And then is heard no more; it is a tale
Told by an idiot, full of sound and fury,
Signifying nothing.

Orson Welles as Macbeth, 1948

In the same act, Lady Macbeth walks in her sleep trying desperately to remove imaginary spots of blood on her hands.

Out, damned spot! out, I say! One; two: why, then 'tis time to do't. Hell is murky! Fie, my lord – fie! a soldier, and afeard? What need we fear who knows it, when none can call our power to account? Yet who would have thought the old man to have had so much blood in him? . . . The Thane of Fife has a wife: where is she now? What, will these hands ne'er be clear? No more o' that, my lord, no more o' that: you mar all with this starting . . . Here's the smell of the blood still: all the perfumes of Arabia will not sweeten this little hand. Oh! oh! oh!

Anastasia Hille as Lady Macbeth at the National Theatre, 1993

What might bring a man and a woman to this state of madness and despair?

What actions or events in their lives might have brought them to this?

- Working in a group, speculate on these questions before you move on.

In order to answer the questions on the previous page more fully, you will need to have a firm grasp of the sequence of events through which the tragedy of these two characters is explored. This is called the **narrative structure** of the play.

THE STORY

- Working in pairs, read through the following summary of the play. Take about ten minutes and try to memorise the main actions of the characters and the events. Then, close the book and see if you can tell each other the story. Check your accuracy when you have finished.

SUMMARY

1   On a desolate heath in Scotland, three witches discuss their plans. They agree to meet again later on that day, in order to speak to a man named 'Macbeth'.

2   News of Scotland's victory in battle reaches the King, Duncan. He hears of the bravery of Macbeth and Banquo and tells a nobleman, Ross, to go to Macbeth and give him the title of 'Thane of Cawdor' as a reward. The man who used to hold this title has been found to be a traitor, and is to be executed.

3   The witches meet Macbeth and Banquo. They amaze Macbeth by calling him 'Thane of Cawdor' and saying that sometime in the future he will himself be King. They tell Banquo he will be the father of Kings, but vanish when Macbeth tries to question them.

4   Ross then enters and tells Macbeth that he is now Thane of Cawdor – news that disturbs him, as the prophecies are proving to be true…

5   When Macbeth and Banquo are welcomed by King Duncan, he thanks them deeply and then names Malcolm, his son, as his heir. Macbeth admits, to himself, that this is an obstacle to his own ambition. He leaves to go home to Inverness, to prepare for the King's visit.

6   At Inverness, Lady Macbeth learns of all these events and plans to persuade her husband to kill the King that night. When Macbeth arrives she begins to suggest this, and then welcomes Duncan into their castle.

7   Macbeth tries to prepare himself for the murder, debating with himself, and then his wife. Cleverly, she persuades him to do it.

8   In the middle of the night, Macbeth nervously waits for the signal to perform the deed. A little while later, Lady Macbeth wonders if all has gone as planned, reacting to every sound. Macbeth joins her when he has killed the King, but she has to return the dagger used in the murder, as he refuses to return to the scene.

9   Macduff, another nobleman, arrives at the castle, and soon discovers the murdered King. In his panic, Macbeth kills Duncan's attendants and claims that he believed them to be responsible for the King's murder. However, Malcolm and Donaldbain, the King's sons, are suspicious, and leave secretly.

10 Macbeth becomes King, but fears Banquo. He hires two murderers to kill him, but does not share the details of this with his wife, even though she has noticed his troubled mind.

11 Banquo is killed, but his son, Fleance, escapes.

12 At a banquet in the palace that night, Macbeth is haunted by the ghost of Banquo, and all the guests notice his strange behaviour. Lady Macbeth tries to calm him. Others are now becoming suspicious too, and Malcolm and Macduff are in England, gathering support against Macbeth.

13 The witches are seen round a cauldron, and when Macbeth joins them they call up apparitions to tell him whether he has anything to fear in the future. He is still not satisfied and so decides to have Macduff's family murdered and his castle seized.

14 In England, Macduff and Malcolm discuss Macbeth. They receive news of these terrible deaths and plan to gather an army against Macbeth.

15 In the palace in Scotland, Lady Macbeth is seen sleepwalking, distressed and seriously disturbed by her memories.

16 Meanwhile, Macbeth tries to convince himself that he cannot be conquered, and talks about his wife's illness. The opposing army, led by Malcolm and Macduff, gathers nearby.

17 Macbeth is told of Lady Macbeth's death, expresses his despair and prepares for battle.

18 As the battle continues, the clever plans of Malcolm's army are revealed and Macbeth eventually realises that the witches' last prophecies have been fulfilled. He challenges Macduff, determined to fight to the death.

19 Macduff kills him and brings his severed head to Malcolm, the new King of Scotland.

Derek Jacobi as Macbeth and Cheryl Campbell as Lady Macbeth at the Barbican, 1993

This activity is designed to help you explore the events by using some of the actual words of the characters themselves.

- Give each person in your class one of the following quotations (right) to read aloud. Allow some time to become familiar with the words. You might experiment by reading aloud in a variety of ways. Whisper the words to each other, recite them all at the same time, or read them aloud one by one, varying the tone of voice you use according to the meaning.

- Use your knowledge of the narrative structure of the play to decide on a possible order for these quotations.

- Finally, present the quotations as a whole group by reciting the lines in their correct order to tell the story of Macbeth.

'For brave Macbeth – well he deserves that name'

'The Queen, my Lord, is dead'

'And fill me from the crown to the toe, top-full of direst cruelty'

'Malcolm and Donalbain, the King's two sons, are stolen away and fled'

'I will tomorrow to the weird sisters'

'Yet I do fear thy nature, it is too full o' the milk of human kindness'

'Behold where stands the usurper's head'

'Your castle is surpris'd, your wife and babes savagely slaughtered'

'All hail, Macbeth, that shalt be King hereafter'

'What is it she does now? See how she rubs her hands'

'I'll fight till from bones my flesh be hacked'

'I have done the deed'

'Ring the alarum bell, murther and treason'

'Banquo, thy soul's flight, if it find Heaven, must find it out tonight'

'But screw your courage to the sticking place and we'll not fail'

THE FORCES AGAINST MACBETH

Another way of looking at the play is to see it as the story of how the opposition to Macbeth slowly gathers strength until it is powerful enough to overthrow him.

- Study the eight statements on the opposite page and place them in the correct order. Then make a copy of the chart and include each statement beside its correct number to show how and why Macbeth's enemies eventually destroy him.

a The army gathers outside Dunsinane, with Malcolm and Macduff in charge.

b Fleance escapes.

c Malcolm suggests cutting branches from Birnam Wood as camouflage.

d Mentieth and Caithness discuss Macbeth as they near his castle.

e Macduff goes home to his castle at Fife, and not to the coronation.

f Duncan's sons flee the castle, Malcolm to England, Donalbain to Ireland.

g Macduff has joined Malcolm in England and is gathering support.

h Macduff learns of his family's death, and plans revenge.

Battle won. Macbeth honoured by King Duncan.

Macbeth decides to kill Duncan.

1	

Macbeth is crowned King.

2	

Death of Banquo. Fleance escapes.

3	

4	

Macbeth visits the witches again,
receives news of Macduff and arranges
the deaths of Lady Macduff and her children.

5	

Lady Macbeth walks in her sleep.

6	

7	

Macbeth prepares for battle, convinced he
cannot be killed.

8	

Macbeth told that Birnam Wood is moving,
and hears of his wife's death.

Battle commences. Macduff kills Macbeth. Malcolm is the new King.

At the beginning of this book, you were asked to consider the reasons why the two central characters, Macbeth and Lady Macbeth, come to such a tragic end. In order to do this, you need to look closely at the script itself. Whilst you will need to read the play as a whole, you will also need to focus on the key scenes which might help you to answer the following questions.

- What are the forces which drive Macbeth to despair?

- To what extent do the witches influence his thoughts and actions?

- To what extent is Lady Macbeth responsible for his tragedy?

- To what extent is only Macbeth himself to blame?

THE WITCHES

What exactly is the role of the witches in the play?

One way of reading any Shakespearian scene closely is to experiment with ways of acting out the text. The witches have always been puzzling, mysterious characters whose role in the play has been hotly debated over the years. Do they have the power directly to influence human behaviour or do they just foretell the future? Do they put ideas into Macbeth's head or do they merely voice the thoughts that are already there?

ACT 1 SCENE 1

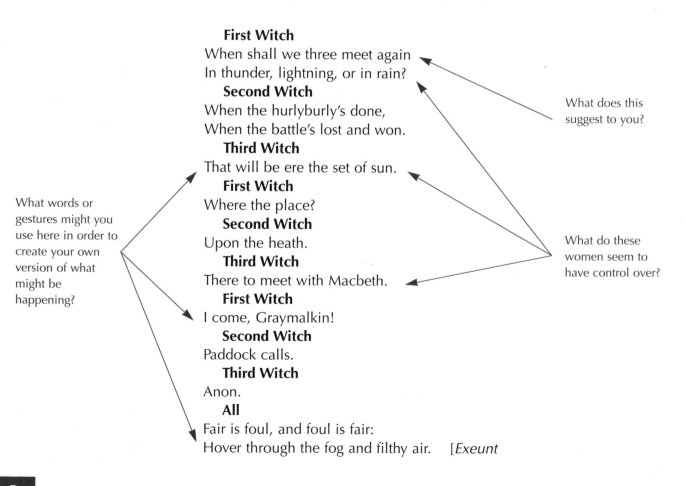

Scene 1 *On the moor. Thunder and lightning. Enter three* Witches

First Witch
When shall we three meet again
In thunder, lightning, or in rain?
Second Witch
When the hurlyburly's done,
When the battle's lost and won.
Third Witch
That will be ere the set of sun.
First Witch
Where the place?
Second Witch
Upon the heath.
Third Witch
There to meet with Macbeth.
First Witch
I come, Graymalkin!
Second Witch
Paddock calls.
Third Witch
Anon.
All
Fair is foul, and foul is fair:
Hover through the fog and filthy air.   [*Exeunt*

What does this suggest to you?

What do these women seem to have control over?

What words or gestures might you use here in order to create your own version of what might be happening?

DIFFERENT READINGS

Here are three ideas for reading the extract:

- Working in a group of three, take a part each and read through quickly, aloud, with no pauses and your heads close together.

- Sit back-to-back in a threesome and recite the words as if you are in a trance, repeating the words in a ritualistic fashion.

- In the same group of three, decide for yourselves what might have led to this encounter. In order to make sense of each of the lines, ask yourself why your character says what she does. Now read the extract aloud, emphasising what it means. Try adding movement to your words by deciding on the method which your witches use to foretell the future. Where in the script would you pause to add these actions?

- How does your view of the witches change with each method of reading?

ACT 1 SCENE 3

The witches eventually meet Macbeth in Act 1 Scene 3. Read this scene again, concentrating on the section before Ross enters.

'MY BLACK AND DEEP DESIRES'

- Work in three groups, one to represent Macbeth, one Banquo and the other the witches.

  Groups one and two should consider the possible reactions and thoughts of Macbeth and Banquo as they hear the first prophecies. The third group should think about the witches, their intentions and their state of mind as they greet the two soldiers on the heath.

- Choose the points in the scene when you think your group might speak their thoughts.

- Present the scene with some of you reading the actual script and others adding the private thoughts of the characters as the scene progresses.

- Still in your groups, discuss to what extent the witches are already influencing Macbeth's thoughts.

ACT 4 SCENE 1

Shakespeare doesn't re-introduce the witches again until Act 4. In some editions you will find that they appear with Hecate in Act 3 Scene 5, but it is probable that this scene was added to the play by somebody other than Shakespeare.

In the next activity, you will be working as a director on Act 4 Scene 1 in order to help you analyse and understand the way the witches and Macbeth interact with each other.

As the director, you will have control over how the audience views and understands the scene. Naturally, your theatre is state-of-the-art and you will be able to plan your production using a computer. On the opposite page is a mock-up of a CD Rom planning programme for theatre direction. The icon bar along the top has all of the special effects you might wish to use.

HELP

THE DIRECTOR'S ROLE

The unseen presence in any theatre performance is that of the Director. In theory, all you need to produce a play is a script and a bunch of actors. In practice, those actors need somebody to help them turn their individual performances into a dramatic experience.

All directors work in different ways. Some are dictators, imposing their will on the actors in order to present their personal vision of what the play is about; some are team leaders, interested in expressing what the cast as a whole think about the play; and some are coaches, concerned to get the best out of each individual performer.

Despite these differences, they probably all have a number of things in common.

- They are responsible for all aspects of the final production of the play, the version that will be seen by the audience on the opening night.

- They will be the final judge of how a character should speak their lines, and what message that will convey to the audience.

- They will have stood in for the audience throughout the rehearsals, communicating to the actors what impression they are giving, holding up a mirror to what is happening on the stage.

- They will have briefed the set and costume designers so that the visual impact of the play is consistent with their view of what it is about.

- They will be responsible for deciding how to light the play, and what sound effects to provide.

- They will organise everything that happens on stage, and much that happens off it.

- They will, in short, have provided an *interpretation* of the words on the page.

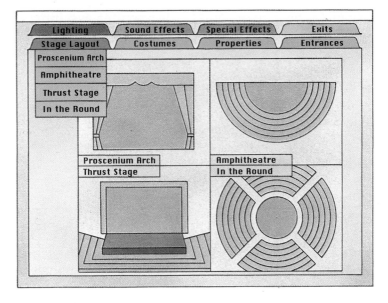

• Working in pairs, start by selecting the kind of theatre that you want from the choice provided:

1 proscenium arch

2 amphitheatre

3 thrust stage

4 theatre in the round.

• Make a list of six key points in Act 4 Scene 1, noting down the most important line(s) of text.

• Use the theatre outline you have chosen to illustrate how you would direct each key moment. You should end up with six outlines. An example of how you might do this for one possible key point is shown below.

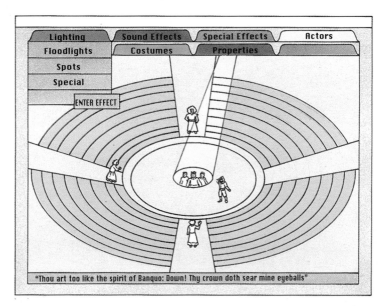

"Thou art too like the spirit of Banquo: Down! Thy crown doth sear mine eyeballs"

Now you have studied each of the witches' scenes, you should be forming some ideas in response to the questions posed at the beginning of the section.

• What is the role of the witches? What are they used for in the play?

• To what extent are they responsible for Macbeth's tragic end?

Three further lines of enquiry might help before you tackle a written assignment.

1 HISTORICAL CONTEXT

It is thought that Shakespeare wrote *Macbeth* for James I, King of both England and Scotland following the death of Elizabeth I. James I was fascinated by witchcraft. He believed his own life had been threatened by witches and, during his reign, he had more women put to death on charges of witchcraft than any other monarch. Clearly, he would have been very interested in the portrayal of the 'weird sisters' in Shakespeare's play.

'SECRET BLACK AND MIDNIGHT HAGS'

- Imagine that you have been summoned by the king in order to explain why you have put on a play that deals with witchcraft. You need to reassure him that you are saying nothing with which he might disagree.

- Write a declaration which proves that the witches in *Macbeth* are evil, with supernatural powers. Support your declaration with quotes from the text. Look at the scroll below for an example of how to begin.

> *Herein Lies Proof*
>
> *They use their wicked art to see into the future; thus breaking the laws of time and nature.... It is suggested that they 'hover through the fog'...*

2 THE POWER OF PROPHECY

One of the 'unnatural' powers the witches seem to possess is that of 'foresight', of being able to tell Macbeth what his future holds.

In groups, discuss the following questions.

- What effect could knowing something about the future have on a person? It might help if you think about this in modern terms. Imagine that you have succeeded in persuading somebody that you have the power to see into the future. This person has real potential and definite hopes and dreams. You decide (guessing) to tell her that she will one day be a famous sportswoman. She believes you. Could this change her life? What might she do?

- Would the events of *Macbeth* have happened without the intervention of the witches? In order to answer this question, you need to look closely at what the witches say to Macbeth and what his thoughts and reactions are.

What exactly do the witches tell Macbeth?	Macbeth's reactions
1 Thane of Glamis	
2 Thane of Cawdor	
3 King hereafter	
4 Beware the Thane of Fife	
5 None of woman born shall harm Macbeth	
6 . . . never vanquished be until Great Birnam wood . . .	

3 THE TESTIMONY OF OTHER CHARACTERS

You need also to look closely at what is said about the witches by other characters. As a class, share out these lines amongst yourselves.

'…so wither'd and so wild'

'…you imperfect speakers'

'…these weird sisters'

'…prophet-like'

'…infected be the air whereon they ride'

'…and damned all those that trust them'

'…the fiend that lies like truth'

'…these juggling fiends'

When everyone has a line, turn the page and try the following activities . . .

- Read your lines at the same time as everyone else.

- Read around the class so that each person takes a turn.

- Create an echo effect by grouping together the people who have the same line (in what way could it be repeated?).

- Choose a simple action which you think is appropriate for your words. For example, 'the fiend that lies like truth' suggests a two-faced, evil creature. How could you represent this through simple, symbolic movement?

- In pairs, read the actual line while your partner voices the thoughts that might lie behind the words. For example, when Macbeth describes the witches as 'prophet-like', he is probably thinking 'they seem to have real power and vision, I'm sure they can see into the future.

COURSE WORK

You should now be able to complete a written assignment based on the question:

- What is the role of the witches and to what extent are they responsible for Macbeth's tragic end?

HELP

When assessing the part played by any character in a play, it is helpful to consider what they contribute towards:

1 the interest – do they interest the audience? Why?

2 the plot – do they change things? How?

3 the audience's knowledge – what do they reveal?

4 relationships – how do they interact with others?

5 atmosphere – what atmosphere surrounds them and what kind of atmosphere do they create?

6 the themes of the play – how do they help us understand the main ideas explored by the play?

LADY MACBETH

'What might bring a man and a woman to this state of madness and despair?'

The influence of the witches on Macbeth needs also to be judged alongside another powerful force in the play – Lady Macbeth. She is one of Shakespeare's most fascinating characters, and her part has been played by some of the world's greatest actresses. Why is she so important?

The first activity is designed to help you get a feeling for the way in which Lady Macbeth changes during the play.

- Work in groups of four or five, with each group taking one of the following key scenes.

The class as a whole are going to present the character of Lady Macbeth through a selection of her own words.

Act 1.v. The reading of the letter

Act 1.vii. Persuading Macbeth

Act 2.ii. The night of the murder

Act 2.iii. The discovery of the murder

Act 3.ii. The conversation before the feast

Act 3.iv. The banquet and Banquo's ghost

Act 5.i. The sleepwalking scene

- In your group, remind yourselves of the scene by reading it through together. Then select a brief quotation each, which you believe shows a crucial moment in the thoughts of Lady Macbeth.

- Taking each scene in order, read all the key quotations aloud to gain an overall impression of Lady Macbeth.

- Finally, consider how these words could be brought to life by the addition of movement, emphasis, tone and expression. You could let one member of your group represent Lady Macbeth and suggest ways in which she could portray the character, or create a tableau or freeze frame which captures the mood of the scene.

You should now have a clear grasp of the overall pattern of development of Lady Macbeth's thoughts in the play. You now need to look very closely at some parts of the key scenes, in order to understand her character in greater depth.

1   THE LETTER

We first meet Lady Macbeth as she reads the letter from her husband.

Scene 5 *Inverness. A room in Macbeth's castle*

Enter Lady Macbeth, *reading a letter*

Lady Macbeth   *'They met me in the day of success; and I have learned by the perfectest report, they have more in them than mortal knowledge. When I burned in desire to question them further, they made themselves air, into which they vanished. Whiles I stood rapt in the wonder of it, came missives from the king, who all-hailed me, "Thane of Cawdor"; by which title, before, these weird sisters saluted me, and referred me to the coming on of time with, "Hail, king that shalt be?" This have I thought good to deliver thee, my dearest partner of greatness, that thou mightest not lose the dues of rejoicing, by being ignorant of what greatness is promised thee. Lay it to thy heart, and farewell.'*

- Read the letter several times to yourself. Try to imagine what a wife in this situation might do with this news. Would she be worried by his ambition and superstitious nature? Would she be proud of his success? Or would she be excited about the prospect of being Queen herself? What alternatives are open to her? Thinking of a variety of reactions will shed light on what Shakespeare actually chose as Lady Macbeth's response, and it will help you to be clear about her. Make a note of what you think.

- In your group, discuss each of the possible reactions that might have occurred to Lady Macbeth.

Here is the view of the actress Sinead Cusack, talking about how she interpreted the scene:

'When she reads that letter, it's almost uncanny for her, because she thinks, "This supernatural news that he's giving me about these three sisters is confirming something that I had already envisioned, that we had already talked about." The letter is almost familiar to her. That experience with the weird sisters – almost as if she knew it would happen. It's as if suddenly everything comes right. Macbeth ought to be Duncan's successor. There was no blood succession in Scotland, the crown was not handed on to the son automatically. Macbeth was the *natural* heir. They had talked about his succession.

Had they discussed the murder of Duncan? I don't think they had. But they had talked about Macbeth being King.

Her own view, the one she'd always held, was that if he wasn't named successor by Duncan then the way through would be to kill. Suddenly, there's the letter with its supernatural news – and the whole universe is endorsing her view, saying to her, "You're right, your vision is correct, and here's the proof." The idea is familiar because she's been through it all in her head already. And here it is; "You're on the right track. You have every right to this. He deserves it."'

• Now read the rest of the scene, concentrating on Lady Macbeth's speeches. As you read them, ask yourself: what response did Shakespeare decide upon in order to reveal her character? Her soliloquy, 'The raven himself is hoarse…' is a famous one. Use this extract from Sinead Cusack's account of playing the part to help you find ways of reading and acting it out, in order to make real sense of the words, images and feelings:

'What I found I had to do in rehearsal, was to clarify absolutely in my head what each of those thoughts reminded of, what situations they were pictures of… you have to isolate each single thought so that it's absolutely clear to you where the picture – where those words – comes from. It took me ages to do that.'

• Start assembling a set of notes on Lady Macbeth by writing down your conclusions about her character from this scene.

2   THE ART OF PERSUASION

At the beginning of Act 1 Scene 7, Macbeth doubts whether he should kill Duncan. Lady Macbeth, however, is determined. Does her determination arise from Macbeth's letter, her personality change or from some inner strength of character?

Make a brief list of all of the ways in which Lady Macbeth tries to put pressure on Macbeth to do what she wants.

In the actual text, Lady Macbeth goes through four phases of persuasion.

Brow-beating
(lines 47–59)

• During this section of the text Lady Macbeth seems to gain the upper hand in the argument. Try out this section in pairs, with Macbeth moving further and further away from his wife. What kind of response does this provoke from her?

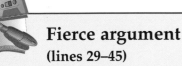

Fierce argument
(lines 29–45)

• In pairs, stand face-to-face and read lines 29–45. During this reading, Macbeth can repeat, 'I dare do all that might become a man' at any stage but he must not look at his wife. Lady Macbeth needs to try to get the better of him by delivering her lines as forcefully as possible and by trying to make Macbeth look at her.

• When you have finished, try thought-tracking each character to gauge their reaction to this approach.

Careful explanation
(lines 60–72)

• Macbeth's final lingering doubt is concerned with the aftermath, 'What if we should fail?' so Lady Macbeth takes him step by step through the plan for the murder. There are plenty of physical actions described in her speech. See how far Lady Macbeth can persuade Macbeth by coaxing him into going through the actions she describes. Try, for example, offering him a knife and, without moving away from the text, see if you can persuade him to accept it.

The final thrust (lines 77–79)

- Try standing all of the Lady Macbeths together, arms raised in victory and all of the Macbeths together, heads bowed. Recite lines 77-79 together, as a group. How would they be said? What other ways can you think of to illustrate this final stage in the argument?

- Count the number of lines spoken by both Macbeth and Lady Macbeth in this scene. What does this tell you about the way in which Lady Macbeth behaves and about their relationship? Who has the power at this time and who is making the decisions? Who is most to blame for killing Duncan?

3 THE MURDER

More is revealed about Lady Macbeth when we see her waiting for Macbeth to complete the murder in Act 2 Scene 2. A close study of this scene will be helped by making notes on the text in order to recognise its dramatic power and the way in which Lady Macbeth's role and her relationship with her husband is changing.

- Read the scene through, paying careful attention to and making notes on the following techniques:

  - characters appearing to hear noises off-stage

  - sentences which contain very few words

  - questions

  - orders.

- Why do you think Shakespeare uses these techniques? What do they show about the emotional states of the characters?

Use your discoveries to complete the following chart:

**Act 2 Scene 2.
The Murder**

Techniques	Emotions	
	Lady Macbeth	*Macbeth*

Consider what Sinead Cusack says about this scene and compare it with your own impressions recorded on the chart.

Sinead Cusack as Lady Macbeth, RSC, 1987

'She is very frightened. She says, "The doors are open." She sees what he is doing, not actually, but in her mind; she is imagining it as it happened and she's beginning to fracture. The line, "Had he not resembled / My father as he slept, I had done't," shocks her. She's trying to hang on. And then she hears a noise, and she goes to the stairs, and then he erupts from the chamber. Panic, panic, panic! She doesn't understand what he's talking about – the language is coming apart!… And then she sees the blood. Now in that moment when she sees the blood, something happens to her gut. For her the sight is horrible. It shocks her, the reality of it. She has imagined the killing, but people who have visions are often shocked by the reality when it comes. When she faces the blood on his hands, it's like a blow to the stomach. And then she gets over it. As an actress I tried to show just a little click in my brain that I could store up to use and refer back to later when I had blood on my own hands.

After that we began talking different languages. We, who had needed to touch each other all the time, grew distant. When he had killed, neither of us wanted to touch the other.

She's saying, "What do you mean, you heard voices?" She's trying to make it practical: well, of course, "There are two lodged together," that's why you heard the voices saying a prayer… but she realises he's gone somewhere that she doesn't understand; she can't bring him back. It's as if she's seeing him drifting, drifting, she's trying to pull him back but he won't come.'

What new things have you discovered about Lady Macbeth's character? What do you think of the way she handles Macbeth? What does this say about her understanding of her husband? Is she terrified of losing him or humiliating him?

4   PUBLIC AND PRIVATE

Only two scenes now remain to show the changing relationship between Lady Macbeth and her husband: a brief conversation just after Macbeth has hired the murderers (Act 3 Scene 2), and the banquet scene (Act 3 Scene 4).

Cheryl Campbell and Derek Jacobi, Barbican, 1993

• Read each scene looking for Lady Macbeth's public face and her private thoughts. Summarise them in a chart like the one below.

Scene	Public face	Private thoughts
Act 3 Scene 2		
Act 3 Scene 4		

• Finally, use your discoveries to experiment with reading these scenes. Think particularly about the spaces between Macbeth and Lady Macbeth – where would they stand in relation to one another?

• During the banquet scene, at which points is Lady Macbeth speaking only to her husband, and when is she speaking generally to her guests?

5   SLEEP WALKING

In the last of Lady Macbeth's scenes (Act 5 Scene 1), Shakespeare shows her walking in her sleep, voicing her nightmares.

Lady Macbeth's actual words are:

Yet here's a spot.

…

Out, damned spot! Out, I say! one; two: why, then 'tis time to do't. Hell is murky! Fie, my Lord – fie! A soldier, and a'feared? What need we fear who knows it, when none shall call our power to account? Yet who would have thought the old man to have had so much blood in him?

…

The Thane of Fife had a wife: where is she now? What, will these hands ne'er be clean? No more o' that my lord, no more o'that: you mar all with this starting.

…

Here's the smell of the blood still: All the perfumes of Arabia will not sweeten this little hand. Oh! Oh! Oh!

…

Wash your hands, put on your nightgown, look not so pale. I tell you yet again, Banquo's buried; he cannot come out on's grave.

…

To bed, to bed: there's knocking at the gate. Come, come, come, come, give me your hand. What's done cannot be undone. To bed, to bed, to bed.

- After you have read this scene, concentrate only on the quotations above. Which phrases are directed towards Macbeth? What does this tell us about Lady Macbeth?

- Now relate each comment made by her in this scene to a real conversation or event earlier on in the play. Look particularly at Act 2 Scene 2 and Act 3 Scene 2. Which moments in the play most haunt her and why?

COURSE WORK SUGGESTIONS

Go back to the questions asked on page 3. What has happened to the Lady Macbeth you encountered at the beginning of the play? Using the notes you have compiled about Lady Macbeth, you should be able to tackle any of the following questions as a course work assignment.

1   *What sort of a person is Lady Macbeth? Think about how she seems at the beginning of the play and how much is revealed by the end. Do you feel any sympathy for her?*

2   *What is Lady Macbeth's main purpose in the play? How does Shakespeare use her to create tension and dramatic effect?*

3   *To what extent is Lady Macbeth to blame for Macbeth's tragedy?*

As an oral activity, you might wish to try the following task:

- Prepare yourself, by using your notes and discussing ideas with a partner, to be hot-seated as Lady Macbeth. You will be asked to account for your actions and to explain your innermost feelings.

MACBETH

*'What might bring a man and a woman to this state of
madness and despair?'*

You have studied Macbeth's reaction to the
witches and his relationship with his wife. Now
it is time for you to look more closely at Macbeth
himself. In order to understand his eventual
despair, and trace how much he is in control of
his own destiny, you need to look at the way
Shakespeare presents his character in the play.

Here may you see
the tyrant

'thou play'dst
most foully for't'

'Each new morn
New widows
howl, new
orphans cry'

'This tyrant,
whose sole name
blisters our
tongues
Was once
thought honest'

'Black Macbeth'

'Not in the
legions of horrid
hell can come a
devil more
damn'd
In evils to stop
Macbeth'

'I grant him bloody,
Luxurious, avaricious,
false, deceitful,
Sudden, malicious,
smacking of every sin
That has a name'

'Devilish Macbeth'

'this fiend'

'Some say he's mad;
others, that lesser hate him
Do call it valiant fury'

'hell-hound'

'coward'

'this dead butcher and
his fiend-like queen'

CHRONICLE OF THE DEEDS OF THE TYRANT

◊ Murder of the gracious Duncan King of Scotland

◊ Murder of the king's attendants

◊ Arranged murder of Banquo, and attempted murder of his son, Fleance

◊ Arranged murder of Lady Macduff and her children

◊ Murder, during battle, of the brave son of Siward, our trusted friend.

'OUR RARER MONSTER'

- Firstly, consider how Macbeth is summed up by other characters in the play, through their actual words.

- At the end of the last act, Macduff says to Macbeth,

We'll have thee, as our rarer monsters are,
Painted upon a pole, and underwrit,
'Here may you see the tyrant.'

Is this a fair judgement of Macbeth?

The following quotations show how Macbeth's state of mind gradually changes from the first glimmers of ambition to the utter despair of the final scenes.

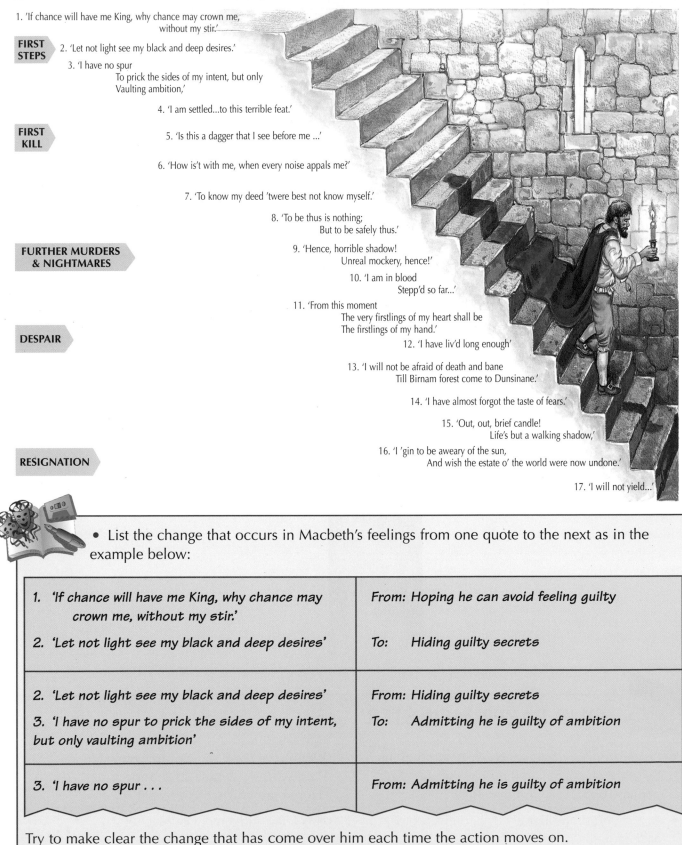

1. 'If chance will have me King, why chance may crown me,
                                         without my stir.'

FIRST STEPS

2. 'Let not light see my black and deep desires.'

3. 'I have no spur
      To prick the sides of my intent, but only
      Vaulting ambition,'

4. 'I am settled...to this terrible feat.'

FIRST KILL

5. 'Is this a dagger that I see before me ...'

6. 'How is't with me, when every noise appals me?'

7. 'To know my deed 'twere best not know myself.'

8. 'To be thus is nothing;
      But to be safely thus.'

FURTHER MURDERS & NIGHTMARES

9. 'Hence, horrible shadow!
      Unreal mockery, hence!'

10. 'I am in blood
      Stepp'd so far...'

11. 'From this moment
      The very firstlings of my heart shall be
      The firstlings of my hand.'

DESPAIR

12. 'I have liv'd long enough'

13. 'I will not be afraid of death and bane
      Till Birnam forest come to Dunsinane.'

14. 'I have almost forgot the taste of fears.'

15. 'Out, out, brief candle!
      Life's but a walking shadow,'

16. 'I 'gin to be aweary of the sun,
      And wish the estate o' the world were now undone.'

RESIGNATION

17. 'I will not yield...'

• List the change that occurs in Macbeth's feelings from one quote to the next as in the example below:

1. 'If chance will have me King, why chance may crown me, without my stir.'	From: Hoping he can avoid feeling guilty
2. 'Let not light see my black and deep desires'	To: Hiding guilty secrets
2. 'Let not light see my black and deep desires'	From: Hiding guilty secrets
3. 'I have no spur to prick the sides of my intent, but only vaulting ambition'	To: Admitting he is guilty of ambition
3. 'I have no spur . . .	From: Admitting he is guilty of ambition

Try to make clear the change that has come over him each time the action moves on.

In three famous soliloquies Shakespeare allows Macbeth to express his very human doubts and fears.

'IF IT WERE DONE...'

The first, in Act 1 Scene 7, shows Macbeth seriously considering whether or not to kill Duncan.

Scene 7 *A room in Macbeth's castle. Music and torches. Servants, carrying dishes for a feast, hurry across the stage. Then enter Macbeth*

Macbeth
If it were done, when 'tis done, then 'twere well
It were done quickly; if th' assassination
Could trammel up the consequence, and catch,
With his surcease, success; that but this blow
Might be the be-all and the end-all – here,
But here, upon this bank and shoal of time,
We'd jump the life to come. But in these cases,
We still have judgement here; that we but teach
Bloody instructions, which, being taught, return
To plague the inventor; this even-handed justice
Commends the ingredients of our poison'd chalice
To our own lips. He's here in double trust:
First, as I am his kinsman and his subject,
Strong both against the deed; then, as his host,
Who should against his murderer shut the door,
Not bear the knife myself. Besides, this Duncan
Hath borne his faculties so meek, hath been
So clear in his great office, that his virtues
Will plead like angels, trumpet-tongu'd, against
The deep damnation of his taking-off;
And pity, like a naked new-born babe,
Striding the blast, or heaven's cherubin, hors'd
Upon the sightless couriers of the air,
Shall blow the horrid deed in every eye,
That tears shall drown the wind. I have no spur
To prick the sides of my intent, but only
Vaulting ambition, which o'er-leaps itself
And falls on the other.

- There are five sentences in this speech. Identify where they begin and end.

- In pairs, call each other **A** and **B**. Read the speech aloud with **A** taking each sentence that presents an argument in favour of killing Duncan, and **B** taking the sentences in which Macbeth is inclined against it.

- Put your argument into modern English.

- Turn your modern version into more of a dialogue, adding arguments on behalf of both points of view.

- Would a simple 'butcher' consider all of these consequences? What exactly is Macbeth worried about?

'IS THIS A DAGGER...'

While Macbeth is waiting for the signal to kill Duncan in Act 2 Scene 1, he is alone on the stage.

Is this a dagger which I see before me,
The handle toward my hand? Come, let me clutch thee:
I have thee not, and yet I see thee still.
Art thou not, fatal vision, sensible
To feeling as to sight? or art thou but
A dagger of the mind, a false creation,
Proceeding from the heat-oppressed brain?
I see thee yet, in form as palpable
As this which now I draw.
Thou marshall'st me the way that I was going;
And such an instrument I was to use.
Mine eyes are made the fools o' the other senses,
Or else worth all the rest: I see thee still;
And on thy blade and dudgeon gouts of blood,
Which was not so before. There's no such thing:
It is the bloody business which informs
Thus to mine eyes. Now o'er the one half-world
Nature seems dead, and wicked dreams abuse
The curtain'd sleep; witchcraft celebrates
Pale Hecate's offerings; and wither'd murder,
Alarum'd by his sentinel, the wolf,
Whose howl's his watch, thus with his stealthy pace,
With Tarquin's ravishing strides, toward his design
Moves like a ghost. Thou sure and firm-set earth,
Hear not my steps, which way they walk, for fear
Thy very stones prate of my whereabout,
And take the present horror from the time,
Which now suits with it. Whiles I threat, he lives:
Words to the heat of deeds too cold breath gives.
                                        [A bell rings
I go, and it is done; the bell invites me.
Hear it not, Duncan; for it is a knell
That summons thee to heaven, or to hell.   *[Exit*

The question that Macbeth is asking himself in this speech is one that is central to the play. Is he leading or being led? Does the dagger represent something in his mind or is it conjured up by evil forces that are manipulating him?

- Working on your own, look at the first 17 lines only. Make a note of those parts of the speech where Macbeth seems convinced that he is being driven by evil forces, and those parts where he dismisses the hallucinations as nothing more than a reflection of his own fears. Does he finally settle the argument one way or the other?

- In the second half of the speech from 'Now o'er the one half world...', Macbeth describes himself moving towards Duncan across a nightmarish landscape. List each of the images that he describes and make a note of what this tells us about how Macbeth views what he is doing. For example:

Image	Feeling
Nature seems dead	Duncan's death is unnatural
People can't sleep because of wicked dreams	The act will haunt him and deprive him of sleep

Jonathan Pryce as Macbeth, RSC, 1987

'TO BE THUS IS NOTHING...'

Just before Macbeth arranges the murder of
Banquo, he reveals the extent of his unrest. Even
though he is king, he has gained no peace of
mind.

> To be thus is nothing:
> But to be safely thus. Our fears in Banquo
> Stick deep, and in his royalty of nature
> Reigns that which would be fear'd: 'tis much he dares,
> And, to that dauntless temper of his mind,
> He hath a wisdom that doth guide his valour
> To act in safety. There is none but he
> Whose being I do fear; and under him
> My genius is rebuk'd, as, it is said,
> Mark Antony's was by Caesar. He chid the sisters
> When first they put the name of king upon me,
> And bade them speak to him; then, prophet-like,
> They hail'd him father to a line of kings.
> Upon my head they plac'd a fruitless crown,
> And put a barren sceptre in my grip,
> Thence to be wrench'd with an unlineal hand,
> No son of mine succeeding. If't be so,
> For Banquo's issue have I fil'd my mind;
> For them the gracious Duncan have I murder'd;
> Put rancours in the vessel of my peace
> Only for them; and mine eternal jewel
> Given to the common enemy of man,
> To make them kings, the seed of Banquo kings!
> Rather than so, come fate into the list,
> And champion me to th' utterance! Who's there?

In this speech, Macbeth gives a number of different reasons for fearing Banquo.

- Working with a partner, list all of the reasons in rank order, putting at the top those which concern Macbeth most.

- What clues did you find in the speech itself to help you decide the order in which to place his concerns?

In the latter part of the play, Shakespeare gives the audience glimpses into the darkness of Macbeth's mind. Read through the following short extracts.

> I have liv'd long enough: my way of life
> Is fall'n into the sere, the yellow leaf;
> And that which should accompany old age,
> As honour, love, obedience, troops of friends,
> I must not look to have; but, in their stead,
> Curses, not loud but deep, mouth-honour, breath,
> Which the poor heart would fain deny, and dare not.

> I am in blood.
> Stepp'd in so far, that, should I wade no more,
> Returning were as tedious as go o'er.

> I have almost forgot the taste of fears.
> The time has been my senses would have cool'd
> To hear a night-shriek, and my fell of hair
> Would at a dismal treatise rouse and stir
> As life were in't. I have supp'd full with horrors;
> Direness, familiar to my slaughterous thoughts,
> Cannot once start me.

> I 'gin to be aweary of the sun,
> And wish the estate o' the world were now undone.
> Ring the alarum-bell! Blow, wind! come, wrack!
> At least we'll die with harness on our back.
> I will not yield,

> To kiss the ground before young Malcolm's feet,
> And to be baited with the rabble's curse.
> Though Birnam wood be come to Dunsinane,
> And thou oppos'd, being of no woman born,
> Yet I will try the last. Before my body
> I throw my warlike shield: lay on, Macduff,
> And damn'd be him that first cries, 'Hold, enough!'
>
> *[Exeunt, fighting*

- In putting these words into Macbeth's mouth, does Shakespeare succeed in making you feel some compassion for him?

- Which of the words on the right might accurately be used to describe Macbeth at this point in the play?

Despairing   dulled   jaded   depressed
bored   resigned   reckless   remorseful
angry   traumatised   aggressive   cowed
destructive   drained   suicidal   self-pitying
defeated

TRAGEDY

Several of Shakespeare's plays are called 'Tragedies', and *Macbeth* is one of them. The notion of a tragedy began with the plays of Ancient Greece and has been used and re-interpreted throughout the history of literature. In Shakespeare's day, there were particular elements common to each of these plays.

A TRAGEDY
- A play that ends with the death of the central character
- A play that deals with universal and serious themes
- A play which signals to the audience that the final outcome is inevitable

A HERO
- A central character
- A character with admirable qualities
- A person with whom the audience can identify, who is human
- A person who influences others and has power

- Discuss in what ways the play *Macbeth* fits the definition of 'Tragedy'.

- In groups of three, prepare ideas to support the argument that Banquo and Lady Macbeth could also be called 'heroes', as well as Macbeth. Each of you will put forward the argument for one character.

A TRAGIC HERO

- A hero whose status means that his downfall will be significant, affecting many people
- A hero whose suffering reveals essential truths about humanity
- A hero whose greatness of character and talent are tragically wasted through circumstance
- A hero whose personality contains a 'tragic flaw': a fatal weakness which leads to destruction
- A hero who finds some degree of release and resignation when facing death

- Use these characteristics to assess the character and role of Macbeth in the play. Write them in the centre of a large piece of paper and surround them with examples from the text that support his role as tragic hero.

- Who would you name as the tragic heroes of the 20th century? You might think about people in: the news, sport, politics or religion… or fictional characters from books, plays, films, television, soap operas…

Now you have studied the way Macbeth's character is revealed, could he, in your opinion, be called a 'tragic hero'?

HELP

Planning and writing a course work assignment

The secret of writing a good course work assignment is to make sure that you have researched the topic and drafted your essay very carefully. You need to go through the following stages:

Title:

Planning

Collecting Information

Drafting

Correcting and Improving

Final Draft

An example is provided below to show how this might work in practice.

Title:
Study the scenes between Macbeth and Lady Macbeth at the beginning of the play. How exactly does Macbeth arrive at the decision to murder Duncan?

Planning
- Introduction
- Macbeth's initial state of mind
- Act 1 Scene 5
  Lady Macbeth's reactions
- Her first words

Collecting Information
- Re-read scenes in pairs
- Note who speaks most and the arguments used
- Look for aggressive language/passive language
- List images used by Lady Macbeth

Drafting
- Sort ideas into paragraph headings
- Link relevant quotes to points made to provide evidence
- Expand points by adding further comments and explanations
- Make sure each point is covered

Correcting and Improving
- Check introduction and conclusion. Are they clear?
- Do paragraphs link well?
- Are enough quotes included?
- Is your punctuation and spelling accurate?
- Does it make sense? Re-read closely.

REVISION EXERCISES

A number of questions have been asked throughout this unit which are summarised below. Any of them would provide an appropriate starting point for a piece of course work about *Macbeth*.

- **Written course work**

    1 'What might bring a man and a woman to this stage of madness and despair? What actions and events in their lives have brought them to this?'

    2 'What are the forces which drive Macbeth?'

    3 'To what extent do the witches influence Macbeth's thoughts and actions?'

    4 'To what extent is Lady Macbeth responsible for this tragedy?'

    5 'To what extent is Macbeth responsible for his own downfall?'

    6 'Is it a fair judgement to say that Macbeth is simply a "butcher"?'

    7 'Is Macbeth a tragic hero?'

- **Oral course work**

    Present your case regarding who is responsible as part of a whole group trial scene investigating the death of King Duncan.